G000291596

Southern Steam *Finale*

By Barry J. Eagles

For Ernest (Ernie) Bartlett

First Published 2002   ISBN 0 946184 94 1

Front cover: Standard class '4' No. 75077 drifts past Lyndhurst Road in the New Forest on 12th June 1967. No. 75077's full details are on page 47. Photo by Barry. J. Eagles

Back cover: 'Battle of Britain' Class No. 34064 *Fighter Command* heads a van train out of Southampton Docks. The *Capetown Castle,* in the background, is unloading cargo from South Africa. *Fighter Command* was built at Brighton in July 1947 and fitted with a Giesl oblong ejector in May 1962. Photo taken on 28th March 1966 by Barry J Eagles.

Frontispiece: 'Battle of Britain' Pacific No. 34089 *602 Squadron* waits at Fareham to take over the Railway Correspondence and Travel Societies Farewell to Southern Steam tour. Photo taken on 18 June 1967 by Barry J Eagles.

Published By

Waterfront

A Division of Kingfisher Productions
The Dalesmade Centre, Watershed Mill, Settle,
North Yorkshire BD24 9LR

Printed by The Amadeus Press, Cleckheaton, West Yorkshire

Foreword

It is 35 years since the end of steam on the Bournemouth line, which I can fortunately still vividly remember. The garden at the house of my maternal grandmother backed onto the Bournemouth main line, approximately half way between Southampton Central and Millbrook Stations. At an early age I fell in love with steam and particularly the engines of the Southern Railway as well as its constituent companies. I would sit in my push chair and listen to the three-cylindered rasping exhaust and middle 'c' whistle of a Bulleid Pacific as it departed from Southampton Central and then watch it pass by with its train, a vision of malachite green loveliness. My uncle Ernie to whom I have dedicated this book, would send me to Sparks, the corner shop, to get bottles of Tizer or Jusoda to quench our thirst in the hot dry summers with Wagon Wheels for sustenance. As a reward he would give me ten shillings and sixpence (52 /2p) to buy the latest Ian Allan Combined Volume. I would then disappear to the bottom of the garden with its chain link fence, covered with convolvulus, to underline the 'cops' in my treasured book. By the age of nine I knew all the named engines of the Southern by heart. I could put a name to every named engine's number, not exactly a useless past time as I developed a memory that could remember historical dates and geographical places, which kept me at the top of the class in those subjects at school! In between the trains, I would read of the latest adventures of Dan Dare in his battle with the Mekon, in the Eagle comic. In the centre would be a superb coloured cutaway drawing of a transport subject by L Ashwell-Wood. I would look forward to a centrefold of a steam locomotive and I soon learnt all about the workings and parts of my beloved steam locomotives.

Through my interest in railways I bought a camera in 1962 and started photographing trains on Kodachrome slide film. By 1964 I had saved £100 to buy a Pentax single lens reflex camera, a good investment with its superb lens. With my Bell and Howell cine camera, Grundig portable reel-to-reel tape recorder and duffle bag, I looked like a portable Christmas tree. This was all unfortunately to come to an end with the Bournemouth line electrification. As from the 10th July 1967 motorised carriages would replace the steam locomotive. From January 1966 until the end of steam all my spare time would be spent filming and tape recording steam locomotives and their trains.

During those last days I was working in the Southampton Mercantile Marine office, involved in the engagement and discharge of ships' crews. My office was next to the Canute Road crossing in Southampton Docks. This gave me a panoramic view of the Ocean Dock, where I could watch the *Queen Mary* and *Queen Elizabeth* arrive and depart. It was fascinating to watch the steam burst out of the Queens' mighty steam horns, with the sound reaching me a second later. The Cunarder Boat Train would wind its way through the docks on its journey to Waterloo. Many goods trains would whistle for the Canute Road Crossing, followed by the clanging of the crossing keepers' hand bell. Some of those Dockland photographs are in this book.

July the 9th 1967 came all too soon and it was with great sadness I witnessed the final day. There was another year of steam in the northwest, but Southern steam was no more. I, along with a lot of other enthusiasts, wondered what we were going to do with our free time; some got involved with sports, and others even discovered girls!

I turned my camera to photographing steam engines that were still working in collieries, power stations and other industrial locations, as well as ocean liners and later, after I got married, I started travelling to Zimbabwe, South Africa and to the Indian sub-continent, where steam engines were in every day use. With a few exceptions, these have all now disappeared. However, all has not been lost, because as I write this in May 2002, I can still visit the same house between Millbrook and Southampton Central stations, and occasionally, I can listen to the three-cylindered rasping exhaust and middle 'c' whistle as 'Merchant Navy' Pacific No. 35005 *Canadian Pacific* passes by with its train of green carriages, observed by my uncle Ernie and myself.

Barry James Eagles, Chandlers Ford, May 2002

Bulleid 'Merchant Navy' Pacific No. 35023 *Holland-Afrika line* passes its birthplace with a 'down' express. Photo taken 20th April 1967 by Barry J. Eagles.

Introduction

The years 1966 and 1967 were sad for steam railway enthusiasts in the south. The encroaching Bournemouth electrification scheme eroded the number of steam locomotives in service monthly. 1962 had seen the end of Maunsell's magnificent trilogy of Arthurs, Schools and Nelsons. Bulleids Pacifics were still doing sterling work although in most cases, poorly maintained, dirty and with nameplates missing. Various standard types helped the Bulleids maintain services. On the first of January 1966 there were 212 steam locomotives available for service. To these must be added the two USA 0-6-0 tanks, numbers DS237 (30065) and DS238 (30070) and 'C' class 0-6-0 number DS 239 (31592), that shunted Ashford Works in Kent. To the west at Meldon Quarry USA class 0-6-0 tank DS234 (30062) was in use, whilst sister engine DS233 (30061) shunted the Redbridge Sleeper Depot. The Isle of Wight still had 14 Adams '02' 0-4-4 tanks to maintain services for 1966, the last year of steam on the Island.

Many enthusiast's specials were run during this period, bringing 'foreign' engines, such as 'A4s' *Sir Nigel Gresley* and *Kingfisher*, as well as other London and North-Eastern Pacifics such as *Blue Peter* and *Flying Scotsman* to the area. The official removal of nameplates was done to prevent their unofficial removal by souvenir collectors. Most of the Merchant Navy class had one nameplate presented to the shipping company they were named after; similarly 'West Country's' had one of their nameplates presented to their namesakes where possible, as did the Battle of Britains. This did not help the appearance of these engines, along with the loss of number plates and the general filthiness of most locomotives. This obviously depressed many railwaymen and enthusiasts, and fortunately some were determined to alter this. Salisbury locomotive shedmaster, Mr Claud Dare, employed cleaners to clean the engines and an Eastleigh diesel fitter, Ron Cover was also determined to improve things, and stated making replacement numberplates for engine's smokeboxes from soup cans!

The year 1967 opened with just two locomotives in use for engineering duties on the Isle of Wight, whilst on the mainland, 120 locomotives remained allocated to the following sheds, Nine Elms (27), Guildford (13), Eastleigh (33), Salisbury (12), Bournemouth (21) and Weymouth (14). Plus the four USA tanks in departmental use.

By July 1967 only 72 steam locomotives were in service - 24 at Nine Elms, 9 at Guildford, 21 at Eastleigh, 3 at Salisbury and 15 at Bournemouth. Three USA 0-6-0 tanks remained in departmental stock. Both '02s' on the Isle of Wight had been withdrawn, but fortunately one, W24 *Calbourne,* was bought for preservation.

After July 9th, engines were towed to the scrap yards of South Wales from the depots where they had been withdrawn. The unlucky ones were cut up at Cashmores and Buttigiegs, both of Newport, and fed to the South Wales furnaces. Fortunately several engines survived the holocaust after several years in the scrapyard at Barry and some are even in use on the main line and preserved railways today.

Bulleid 'West Country' Pacific No. 34047 *Callington* departs from Southampton Central with the 'down' Bournemouth Belle. This prestigeous service was scheduled to be diesel-hauled from the beginning of 1967, although steam did appear on it from time to time when a diesel was unavailable. *Callington* was built at Brighton in November 1946, and was rebuilt at Eastleigh in October 1958. She was withdrawn just before the end of steam in June 1967 from Nine Elms shed after running 845,991 miles. Buttigiegs of Newport broke her up in September 1968. Photo taken on 15th November 1965 by Barry J Eagles.

Bulleid 'West Country' Pacific No. 34005 *Barnstaple* steams past Shawford station on an 'up' Waterloo express. *Barnstaple* was built at Brighton in July 1945 and was the first Light Pacific to be rebuilt at Eastleigh in June 1957. She was withdrawn in September 1966 from Eastleigh shed but reinstated on 10th December for the Christmas parcels traffic. After running 837,332 miles she was broken up by Buttigiegs of Newport in 1968.
Photo taken on 22nd November 1965 by Barry J Eagles.

Standard class '5' 4-6-0 No. 73092 nears Shawford Station with an express for Bournemouth. No. 73092 was built at Derby in October 1955, one of 130 built there. Built new for the London Midland Region, she was transferred to Eastleigh in April 1965. This Standard class '5' was to work two early morning turns on the last weekday of steam on 7th July before remaining at Weymouth MPD ready for withdrawal three days later. Withdrawn in July 1967 from Weymouth shed and broken up at Cashmores, Newport in January 1968. Photo taken on 22nd November 1965 by Barry J Eagles.

'Merchant Navy' Pacific No. 35017 *Belgian Marine*, races through Lyndhurst Road Station with an 'up' express for Waterloo. *Belgian Marine* was built at Eastleigh in April 1945 and allocated to Nine Elms shed. The Belgian minister of communications named her at Victoria Station on 22nd October 1945. *Belgian Marine* was rebuilt at Eastleigh in March 1957. Withdrawn in July 1966 after running 1,017,754 miles and broken up at Buttigiegs, Newport in September 1966. Photo taken on 24th November 1965 by Barry J Eagles.

Standard class '5' 4-6-0 No. 73084 roars under Ashurst Road Bridge with an express for Bournemouth. No. 73084 was built at Derby in June 1955 for the Southern Region. In November 1959, she was named *Tintagel* taking her name from the withdrawn 'King Arthur', No. 30745. Withdrawn in December 1965 and broken up at Birds, Bridgend in April 1966. Photo taken on 24th November 1965 by Barry J Eagles.

'West Country' Pacific No. 34019 *Bideford* steams through a snow-covered Shawford with an 'up' Waterloo express. *Bideford* was built at Brighton in December 1945 and allocated to Exmouth Junction shed. Withdrawn in March 1967 after running 701,316 miles and broken up at Cashmores, Newport in September 1967. Photo taken on 15th January 1966 by Barry J Eagles.

'West Country' Pacific No. 34047 *Callington* storms through Shawford in the deep mid winter. *Callington* was built at Brighton in November 1946 and allocated to Exmouth Jct shed. In October 1958 she was rebuilt at Eastleigh Works. Withdrawn in June 1967 after running 845,991 miles and broken up at Buttigiegs, Newport in September 1968. Photo taken on 15th January 1966 by Barry J Eagles.

Maunsell 'S15' 4-6-0 No. 30837 in immaculate condition hauls the Locomotive Club of Great Britain's 'S15 Commemorative Rail Tour' near Binstead Crossing. No. 30837 was built at Eastleigh in January 1928, one of 25 Maunsell S15's, 20 had been built by Urie, making a class of 45 engines. Withdrawn from Feltham shed in September 1965, No. 30837 had been reinstated for working this special rail tour and was the last of any 'S15' class in service. Broken up at Cashmores, Newport in September 1966. Photo taken on 15th January 1966 by Barry J Eagles.

Merchant Navy' Pacific No. 35028 *Clan Line* stands outside the entrance of Southampton Tunnel bound for Eastleigh shed. Just to the left of the signal, you can see the sign depicting the old Gaumont theatre, now the Mayflower. *Clan Line* was built at Eastleigh in December 1948 and allocated to Bournemouth shed - Lord Rotherwick, Chairman of Clan Line, named her at Southampton Docks on 15th January 1951. She was rebuilt at Eastleigh in October 1959. *Clan Line* became a familiar sight on 'end of steam' railtours and was finally withdrawn in July 1967 after running 794, 391 miles and sold to the Merchant Navy Locomotive Preservation Society in working order. Presently being overhauled at Stewarts Lane. Photo taken on 20th February 1966 by Barry J Eagles.

Maunsell 'N' 2-6-0 No. 31411 heads a special train past Fort Brockhurst on the Gosport branch. No. 31411 was built at Ashford in November 1933, one of 80 'N' class: 30 were built at Ashford and 50 at the Woolwich Arsenal, bought cheaply at £3,962 each, hence their nickname 'Woolworths'. Withdrawn in April 1966 and broken up at Cashmores, Newport in September 1966. Photo taken on 20th February 1966 by Barry J Eagles.

No. 31411 heads tender first across Fareham Bridge with the same special train as seen on page 13. This special train was the Southern Counties Touring Society's Southdown Venturer and had departed from Victoria behind 'West Country' Pacific No. 34013 *Okehampton* and ran via Oxted, Uckfield, Lewes to Brighton, then to Fareham and Gosport and then Gosport to Portsmouth Harbour. *Okehampton* then took the train to London Bridge via Guildford. Photo taken on 20th February 1966 by Barry J Eagles.

USA 0-6-0 tank No. 30069 shunts Banana Vans in Southampton Docks. No. 30069 was built for the United States Army Transportation Corp by the Vulcan Iron Works of Wilkes-Barre USA their Works No. 4425 of 1943. Bought by the Southern Railway for shunting at Southampton Docks. No. 30069 was placed in service in November 1947. 30069 worked up until the end of Southern Steam in July 1967, along with four other USA Tanks. She was broken up at Cashmores Newport in March 1968. Four USA Tanks Nos. 30064, 30065, 30070 and 30072 are preserved. Photo taken 16th March 1967 by Barry J. Eagles.

Standard Class '4' 2-6-0 No. 76026 pilots 'West Country' Pacific No. 34032 *Camelford* out of Southampton Central Station with a train to Bournemouth. No. 76026 was built at Doncaster in December 1953, one of the 50 built there: 45 were built at Horwich and 20 at Derby. Withdrawn in July 1967 and broken up at Cohens, Morriston in September 1967. *Camelford* was built at Brighton in June 1946 and rebuilt at Eastleigh in October 1960. Withdrawn in October 1966 after running 853,398 miles and broken up at Buttigiegs, Newport. This classic location was popular with photographers in the last few years of steam. Photo taken on 20th February 1966 by Barry J Eagles.

Ivatt class '2' 2-6-2 tanks Nos. 41301 and 41284 doublehead the Locomotive Club of Great Britain's 'Dorset Belle' out of Corfe Castle. Both engines were built at Crewe - 41301 in 1952, and 41284 in 1950. 130 were built: 120 at Crewe and 10 at Derby. No. 41301 was withdrawn in October 1966 from Eastleigh shed and broken up by Cohens, Morriston in March 1967. No. 41284 was withdrawn from Nine Elms in March 1967 and broken up at Buttigiegs, Newport in September 1967. Photo taken on 27th February 1966 by Barry J Eagles.

'Merchant Navy' Pacific No. 35028 *Clan Line* heads the 'Dorset Belle' near Wool. *Clan Line* departed from Waterloo with the special and travelled to Wareham via Alton then to Weymouth. Withdrawn from Nine Elms in July 1967, *Clan Line's* details are on page 12.
Photo taken on 20th February 1966 by Barry J Eagles.

'Battle of Britain' Pacific No. 34056 *Croydon* is commendably clean as she awaits her next call to duty. *Croydon* was built at Brighton in February 1947, and rebuilt at Eastleigh in December 1960. She was allocated to Stewarts Lane Shed when new and ended up with two classmates at 70E Salisbury MPD. Withdrawn in May 1967, after running 957,081 miles, and broken up at Cashmores Newport. Three rebuilt and six unrebuilt 'Battle of Britain's' are preserved. Photo taken on 19th February 1967 by Barry J. Eagles.

Ivatt Class '2' 2-6-2 tanks Nos. 41301 and 41284 storm up Upwey Bank with the Dorset Belle. These locomotives had worked the special along the Swanage Branch and were on their way to Bridport and Yeovil Junction where Bulleid Pacific, 'Battle of Britain' No. 34057 *Biggin Hill,* would take the train to Waterloo. Locomotive details on page 17. Photo taken on 20th February 1966 by Barry J Eagles.

'West Country' Class No. 34100 *Appledore* glints in the evening sunlight at Salisbury Station. *Appledore* was built at Brighton in December 1949 and rebuilt at Eastleigh in September 1960. She was allocated to Ramsgate shed when new and lasted until 1st July 1967 at Salisbury. Withdrawn in July 1967 after running 712,916 miles and broken up at Cashmores, Newport in October 1967. Photo taken on 14th July 1966 by Barry J Eagles.

Standard Class '5' 4-6-0 No. 73155 heads past the site of Nursling Station with a train for Salisbury and the West. No. 73155 was built at Doncaster in December 1956 and allocated to Neasden. In December 1962 she was transferred to Eastleigh and then to Guildford in March 1967. Withdrawn in July 1967 at the end of Southern steam, No. 73155 ran in tandem with No. 73118 to Salisbury where it was stored until February 1968 and eventually broken up at Cashmores, Newport a month later. Photo taken on 9th March 1966 by Barry J Eagles.

Two passenger trains on the Bournemouth line meet near Lymington Junction, the junction for the last steam-worked branch line. This connected with the ferries to Yarmouth on the Isle of Wight. A 'Merchant Navy' heads up towards Brockenhurst and Waterloo as a 3-coach local to Bournemouth heads west. Photo taken on 12th March 1966 by Barry J Eagles.

Standard Class '4' 4-6-0 No. 75076 nears Lymington Junction with a train to Bournemouth. No. 75076 was built at Swindon in December 1955, one of eighty built there. Built new for the Southern Region, she was fitted with a double chimney in June 1961. No. 75076 was withdrawn at the end of Southern Steam in July 1967, along with four other Standard Class 4-6-0s. She was broken up at Birds Risca in December 1967. Nos. 75014, 75027, 75029, 75069, 75078 and 75079 have been preserved. Photo taken on 4th February 1967 by Barry J. Eagles.

Standard Class '4' 2-6-4 tank No. 80085 waits to depart Lymington pier. A suitable candidate for one of Ron Cover's 'soup tin number plate's. No. 80085 was built at Brighton in June 1954 and did not transfer to the Southern Region until November 1959 when she was allocated to Bricklayers Arms shed. Withdrawn in July 1967 from Nine Elms shed and broken up at Birds, Risca in February 1968. Several of the class are preserved.
Photo taken on 12th March 1966 by Barry J Eagles.

Standard Class '4' 2-6-4 tank No. 80013 brings the Lymington Branch train into Brockenhurst station, passing Ivatt Class '2' 2-6-2 tank No. 41230 waiting to relieve her. No. 41230 was built at Crewe in 1949, one of the 120 built there: 10 were also built at Derby. Withdrawn in April 1967 and broken up at Cohens, Morriston in September 1967. Photo taken on 10th May 1966 by Barry J Eagles.

Standard Class '4' 2-6-4 tank No. 80013 heads bunker first away from Brockenhurst with a train for Lymington Pier, as depicted by the correct head code disc. No. 80013 was built at Brighton in October 1951, one of 130 built there: 15 were built at Derby and a further 15 at Doncaster. Allocated to the Southern Region and used on the Central Section she was withdrawn in June 1966 and broken up at Kings, Norwich in December 1966. Photo taken on 10th May 1966 by Barry J Eagles.

Ivatt Class '2' 2-6-2 tank No. 41312 catches the winter sun at Bournemouth Shed. No. 41312 was built at Crewe in 1952. These engines replaced many of the 0-4-4 tank locomotives of the 'M7' and 'H' classes on branch passenger workings. One of the last five that survived until the end of Southern steam. This engine has the distinction of hauling the very last steam-hauled train service over the Lymington branch on 2nd April 1967. Withdrawn in July 1967 and sold to Woodham's of Barry. She languished there until August 1974, when she was bought by the Caerphilly Railway Society. No. 41312 has been restored to working order and now resides on the Mid-Hants Railway. Three others Nos. 41241, 41298 and 41313 have also been preserved.
Photo taken on 21st January 1967 by Barry J. Eagles.

'Battle of Britain' Class Pacific No. 34071 *601 Squadron* climbs towards Sway with an express for Bournemouth. *601 Squadron* was built at Brighton in April 1948 and allocated to Dover shed. She was rebuilt at Eastleigh in May 1960 and withdrawn in April 1967 after running 782,028 miles. Broken up at Cashmores, Newport in September 1967. Photo taken on 12th March 1966 by Barry J Eagles.

'Merchant Navy' Pacific, No. 35012 *United States Line*, roars past Lymington Junction with the Lymington Branch train in the background. *United States Line* was built at Eastleigh in March 1949. Admiral Schuirman of the United States Navy named her at Waterloo Station, on 10th April 1945. She was allocated when new to Nine Elms Shed and rebuilt at Eastleigh in February 1957, withdrawn in April 1967 after running 1.134,836 miles. The American Railroad museum at Green Bay had requested her for preservation but this unfortunately fell on deaf ears and she was broken up at Cashmores Newport. Photo taken on 24th September 1966 by Barry J. Eagles.

'Merchant Navy' Class No. 35030 *Elder Dempster Lines* departs from Brockenhurst with a train to Bournemouth. *Elder Dempster Lines* was built at Eastleigh in April 1949, the last of the thirty-strong class to be built. Mr G H Avezathe, a director of the company, named her at Southampton Docks on the 5th June 1950. She was rebuilt at Eastleigh in April 1958. No. 35030 has the distinction of hauling the very last steam passenger train; the 14.07 from Weymouth to Waterloo on 9th July 1967. Withdrawn in July 1967 after running 850,876 miles and broken up at Buttigiegs, Newport. Photo taken on 10th May 1966 by Barry J Eagles.

With just two months before the end of steam on the branch, Standard Class '4' 2-6-4 Tank No. 80146 departs Lymington Town with a train for Brokenhurst. Nos. 80146 was built at Brighton in November 1956, and allocated to the Southern Region for use on the Central Section. Transferred to Bournemouth Shed in December 1963, No. 80146 worked up until the end of Southern Steam in July 1967, along with ten other Standard Class '4' Tanks. She was broken up at Birds Risca. Photo taken on 4th February 1967 by Barry J. Eagles.

'Battle of Britain' Pacific No. 34052 *Lord Dowding*, hauls a lightweight train near Lymington Junction. *Lord Dowding* was built at Brighton in December 1946, and rebuilt at Eastleigh in September 1958. It was allocated to Salisbury Shed when new. One of the last five rebuilt 'Battle of Britains' at the end of Southern steam. *Lord Dowding* headed a perishable train to Westbury and returned light engine to Weymouth on the final day of steam, 9th July 1967. Withdrawn on that date after running 936,502 miles and broken up at Cashmores Newport. Photo taken on 24th September 1966 by Barry J. Eagles.

'West Country' Pacific No. 34023 *Blackmore Vale* departs light engine from Weymouth Shed. *Blackmore Vale* was built at Brighton in February 1946. She was allocated to Ramsgate Shed when new. One of only two unrebuilt 'West Country's' to survive until the end of Southern Steam, the other being No. 34102 *Lapford*. *Blackmore Vale* was withdrawn in July 1967 after running 921,268 miles and sold for preservation, and now works on the Bluebell Railway. Seven rebuilt and four unbuilt 'West Country's' are preserved. Photo taken on 7th May 1967 by Barry J. Eagles.

'West Country' Pacific No. 34004 *Yeovil* stands sentinel on Weymouth Shed. *Yeovil's* nameplate has gone, but the backing plate remains. *Yeovil's* details are on page 37. Photo taken on 7th May 1967 by Barry J. Eagles.

'West Country' Pacific No. 34025 *Whimple* departs Fareham with a Bournemouth train diverted by engineering works. Lines to Eastleigh via Botley disappear to the middle left. *Whimple* was built at Brighton in March 1946 and rebuilt at Eastleigh in November 1957. She worked right up to the end of Southern steam working the 6.54pm Waterloo to Basingstoke train on 8th July 1967. Withdrawn in July 1967 after running 872,938 miles. Stored at Salisbury shed until February 1968 and broken up at Cashmores, Newport a month later. Photo taken on 12th March 1966 by Barry J Eagles.

'West Country' Pacific No. 34004 *Yeovil* approaches Basingstoke. The impressive signal *Yeovil* is passing under is soon to disappear. The replacement signal can be seen above the second coach. *Yeovil* was built at Brighton in July 1945, and rebuilt at Eastleigh in February 1958. She was allocated to Exmouth Junction shed when new. Photo taken on 17th September 1966 by Barry J. Eagles.

A week later a still grubby-looking *Yeovil* rushes through Totton with an 'up' Waterloo express. *Yeovil* was one of the last fourteen rebuilt 'West Country's' at the end of Southern steam, and withdrawn in July 1967 after running 920,972 miles and broken up at Cashmores Newport in October 1967.
Photo taken on 24th September 1966 by Barry J. Eagles.

Standard Class '5' 4-6-0 No. 73043 heads a stopping train across Redbridge Causeway and catches the glint from the evening sunlight. The South Western Tar Distillery at Totton can be seen in the background. No. 73043 was built at Derby in October 1953, and allocated to the London Midland Region. Transferred to Eastleigh Shed in December 1962, she remained at work until the end of Southern Steam along with nine classmates. Withdrawn in July 1967, she was broken up at Cashmores Newport. Photo taken on 15th June 1967 by Barry J. Eagles.'

'Merchant Navy' Class No. 35013 *Blue Funnel* runs into Southampton Central Station. The impressive signal gantry stood here for many years and lasted until the mid-1980s. It is now in the National Collection at York. *Blue Funnel* was built at Eastleigh in February 1945. Mr L Holt named her at Waterloo Station on the 17th April 1945. She was rebuilt at Eastleigh in May 1956. On 26th June 1967 *Blue Funnel* attained a speed on 106 miles per hour in what became steam's finale in the Southern Region. She would go on to double-head with No. 35030 in a rare working from Weymouth on a special on 11th June 1967. Withdrawn in July 1967 after running 1,114,658 miles and broken up at Buttigiegs, Newport in October 1967. Photo taken on 22nd August 1966 by Barry J Eagles.

Nine Elms-shedded Pacific No. 34008 *Padstow*, drifts past Millbrook Signal Box. *Padstow* was built at Brighton in September 1945, and rebuilt at Eastleigh in July 1960. She was allocated to Exmouth Junction Shed when new. Withdrawn in June 1967 after running 961,734 miles and broken up at Buttigiegs Newport. Photo taken on 3rd June 1967 by Barry J. Eagles.

'West Country' Class No. 34037 *Clovelly* departs from Southampton Central with a train for Bournemouth. *Clovelly* was built at Brighton in August 1946 and rebuilt at Eastleigh in March 1958. She was allocated to Stewarts Lane shed when new. One of the last 14 rebuilt 'West Countrys' at the end of Southern steam, *Clovelly* worked the 2.30am Waterloo to Portsmouth train on the 8th July 1967. Withdrawn in that month after running 810,658 miles and broken up at Cashmores, Newport in March 1968. Photo taken on 29th March 1966 by Barry J Eagles.

USA tank No. 30073 shunts in Southampton Docks. The Union Castle liner, *Capetown Castle* is in the background. No. 30073's details are on page 60. The motor vessel *Capetown Castle* had been built by Harland and Wolff of Belfast in 1938. Photo taken on 28th March 1966 by Barry J Eagles.

Standard Class '5' 4-6-0 No. 73093 heads a freight train out of Southampton Docks, passing a Cunard freighter. No. 73093 was built at Derby in November 1955, one of the 130 built there: 42 were built at Doncaster. It was at first allocated to the London Midland Region, and transferred to Eastleigh shed in April 1965. No. 73093 was withdrawn at the end of Southern steam in July 1967, along with 10 other Class '5's. She was broken up at Cashmores, Newport in March 1968. Photo taken on 28th March 1966 by Barry J Eagles.

'Battle of Britain' Pacific No. 34053 *Sir Keith Park* waits to depart Waterloo Station, the London terminus of the South Western Section of the Southern Region. It was a location that saw an influx of interest from enthusiasts trying to capture the last scenes of Bulleid Pacifics leaving here for the South West. *Sir Keith* was built at Brighton in January 1947 and allocated to Salisbury Shed and rebuilt at Eastleigh in November 1958. Withdrawn in October 1965 after running 825,317 miles. Bought by Woodham Brothers of Barry. Resold for preservation and is now awaiting restoration at Sellindge in Kent. Photo taken on the 10th August 1965 by Barry J. Eagles.

Stanier Black '5' 4-6-0 No. 45493 passes under Brokenford Bridge, Totton, with a through train from the north. No. 45493 was built at Derby in 1944, one of 842 Black Fives. These through trains normally ran from Newscastle to Poole and were worked by Great Western 'Halls' from Oxford until 1964. Twenty other members of the class were recorded on these services during 1966. Withdrawn in December 1967 from Carlisle, Kingmoor shed and broken up at Drapers, Hull in April 1968. Photo taken on 30th April 1966 by Barry J Eagles.

Standard Class '4' 4-6-0 No. 75077, proudly displaying its 'Ron Cover' numberplate, roars by Ashurst crossing with a train for Bournemouth. No. 75077 was built at Swindon in December 1955 and fitted with a double chimney in June 1961. Built new for the Southern Region, No. 75077 spent most of her life allocated to Eastleigh Shed. Withdrawn in July 1967, along with 20 other assorted locomotives at Eastleigh and broken up at Kings Norwich. Photo taken on 16th June 1967 by Barry J. Eagles.

Merchant Navy' Pacific No. 35023 *Holland Afrika Line* passes under Brokenford Bridge, Totton, with an express for Bournemouth. *Holland Afrika* was built at Eastleigh in November 1948 and rebuilt there in February 1957. She was allocated to Exmouth Junction shed when new. The managing director of Holland Afrika Line, named the engine at Southampton Docks on the 24th January 1949. One of the last eight 'Merchant Navy's' in service at the end of steam, she hauled the 8.30am Waterloo to Weymouth train arriving eight minutes early on the 8th July 1967. She then hauled the last steam-worked 'up' service back to Waterloo in the afternoon. Withdrawn straight afterwards, after running 941,326 miles and broken up at Buttigiegs, Newport in April 1968.
Photo taken on 19th March 1966 by Barry J Eagles.

'Battle of Britain' class Pacific No. 34087 *145 Squadron* passes Ashurst Crossing with a light weight stopping train to Bournemouth. *145 Squadron* was built at Brighton in December 1948, and rebuilt at Eastleigh in December 1960. She was allocated to Ramsgate Shed when new and was based at 70D Eastleigh at the end. Withdrawn in July 1967, after running 704, 638 miles and broken up at Cashmores Newport. Photo taken on 14th June 1967 by Barry J. Eagles.

Bulleid 'Q1' 0-6-0 No. 33006 heads the Locomotive Club of Great Britain's 'New Forester Railtour' under Brokenford Bridge, Totton, heading for Brockenhurst and Lymington Pier. She had worked the special from Eastleigh to Gosport and Southampton Terminus. No. 33006 was built at Brighton in June 1942, one of the 20 built there: the other 20 being built at Ashford. Nos. 33006, 33020 and 33027 were the last 'Q1's' in service and all were withdrawn in January 1966. No. 33006 had to be reinstated to haul the special and was broken up at Cashmores, Newport in August 1966. Photo taken on 19th March 1966 by Barry J Eagles.

Bulleid' Merchant Navy' Pacific No. 35013 *Blue Funnel* (without its nameplates) passes Ashurst with an 'up' express. *Blue Funnel*'s details are on page 40. Eleven 'Merchant Navy's' are preserved. Photo taken on 21st June 1967 by Barry J. Eagles.

'Merchant Navy' Pacific No. 35007 *Aberdeen Commonwealth* rolls past Ashurst Crossing with the 'up' Channel Islands Boat Express. *Aberdeen Commonwealth* was built at Eastleigh in June 1942. Lord Essendon Chairman of Aberdeen Commonwealth, named her at Victoria Station on 30th July 1942. She was allocated when new to Salisbury Shed, and rebuilt at Eastleigh in May 1958. *Aberdeen Commonwealth*'s last major duty was to work the 5.30pm Weymouth to Waterloo on 6th July 1967 during which she attained 98 mph near Bramshott. Withdrawn in July 1967 after running 1,308,765 miles and broken up at Buttigiegs Newport in April 1968. Photo taken on 13th June 1967 by Barry J. Eagles.

'West Country' Class No. 34004 *Yeovil* roars past Shawford Junction with an 'up' express and yes I did have a lineside permit! *Yeovil*'s details are on page 37. Photo taken on 10th June 1967 by Barry J. Eagles.

Bulleid 'Merchant Navy' Pacific No. 35028 *Clan Line* brings the Channel Island Boat Express past the site of Shawford Junction. Shawford Junction was where the Didcot Newbury and Southampton Line left the Southern's main line. Three weeks later *Clan Line* would haul one of the two BR Southern Steam Finale specials on 2nd July. *Clan Line*'s details are on page 12. Photo taken on 10th June 1967 by Barry J. Eagles.

'West Country' Pacific No. 34032 *Camelford* powers down the Portsmouth main line with an express diverted from the Bournemouth line due to electrification works. The Southern's unique head code disc is for a train from Victoria to Portsmouth via Mitcham Junction. *Camelford's* details are on page 16.
Photo taken on 20th March 1966 by Barry J Eagles.

Above: 'West Country' Pacific No. 34104 *Bere Alston* passes Farlington Junction signal box with another diverted Bournemouth Line express. *Bere Alston* was the last steam locomotive to be built at Eastleigh in April 1950 and by a strange coincidence she was the last one to be rebuilt there in May 1961. She was allocated, when new, to Stewarts Lane shed. Withdrawn in June 1967 after running 678,853 miles and broken up at Buttigiegs, Newport. Photo taken on 20th March 1966 by Barry J Eagles.

Right: Standard Class '5' 4-6-0 No. 73029 doubleheads with 'West Country' Pacific No. 34023 *Blackmore Vale* into Fareham Station, with the Railway Correspondence and Travel Societies Farewell to Southern Steam railtour. They had hauled this tour from Waterloo via Guildford. No. 73029 was built at Derby in January 1952, and allocated to the Western Region. Transferred to the Southern Region after working on the Somerset and Dorset from Bath Shed, she kept her green passenger livery until the end. Withdrawn in July 1967, she was broken up at Cashmores Newport in March 1968. *Blackmore Vale*'s details are on page 34. Photo taken on 18th June 1967 by Barry J. Eagles.

'West Country' Pacifics, Nos. 34023 *Blackmore Vale* and 34108 *Wincanton,* doublehead the Railway Correspondence and Travel Societies Railtour through Totton. They had worked the special from Weymouth and would take it to Salisbury via Eastleigh, where No. 35013 *Blue Funnel* would take the train to Waterloo. *Wincanton* was built at Brighton in April 1950 and rebuilt at Eastleigh in May 1961. She was allocated to Bournemouth Shed when new and withdrawn in June 1967 from Salisbury MPD, after running 808,361 miles, and broken up at Buttigiegs Newport.
Photo taken on 18th June 1967 by Barry J. Eagles.

'Battle of Britain' Pacific No. 34089 *602 Squadron* heads the Railway Correspondence and Travel Societies Special away from Fareham. *602 Squadron* was built at Brighton in December 1948, and rebuilt at Eastleigh in November 1960. It was allocated to Ramsgate shed when new. According to records *602 Squadron* was the last steam locomotive to be repaired at Eastleigh Works being outshopped on 6th October 1966. Withdrawn in July 1967, after running 661,252 miles, and broken up at Cashmores Newport. Photo taken on 18th June 1967 by Barry J. Eagles.'

Above: Nos. 30064 and 30073 cross the Marchwood by-pass with the 'Solent Railtour'. This tour had started from Waterloo behind 'Battle of Britain' No. 34089 for Salisbury. Standard Class 4-6-0 No. 75070 hauled the train to Southampton Ocean Terminal where USA's Nos. 30064 and 30073 took over for a round trip to Fawley and back to Southampton Terminus. No. 75070 then hauled the train to Fareham, where 'U' Class No. 31639 took over for the Gosport Branch. This engine then coupled up with No. 75070 to double head the train back to Waterloo, a good day out! No. 30064 was withdrawn in July 1967 and is now preserved on the Bluebell Railway. No. 30073 was not so lucky, being withdrawn in December 1966 and broken up at Cashmores, Newport in June 1967.

Right: USA 0-6-0 tanks, Nos. 30064 and 30073, trundle across the Redbridge Causeway with the Railway Correspondent and Travel Society's 'Solent Railtour'. The Vulcan Iron Works of Wilkes-Barre USA had built both engines for the United States Army Transportation Corps. No. 30064 was built in 1942 works number 4432 and 30073 was built in 1943 works number 4447. These engines had been obtained from a dump at Newbury Race Course for the bargain prices of £2,500 each, they had been bought for shunting in Southampton Docks. 14 were obtained plus one for spares. Both photos taken on 20th March 1966 by Barry J Eagles.

'Battle of Britain' Class No. 34052 *Lord Dowding* is spotless as it takes the Salisbury line at Redbridge just six days before the last day of steam traction with a trainload of Banana Vans. The damaged stone built Redbridge Locomotive Shed can be seen on the right of the picture. The resident USA shunter had pushed the rear wall out. *Lord Dowding's* details are on page 33. Photo taken on 3rd July 1967 by Barry J. Eagles.

Un-rebuilt Pacific No. 34023 *Blackmore Vale* is spotless as she waits to cross Canute Road to travel light engine to Eastleigh. She was a regular sight in the Southampton and Bournemouth areas in the last few weeks and was seen on various duties including railtours. Behind her is part of the magnificent South Western House. A Ford Cortina is amongst the cars parked on the right. *Blackmore Vales's* details are on page 34.
Photo taken on 16th June 1967 by Barry J. Eagles.

'Battle of Britain' Pacific No. 34090 *Sir Eustace Missenden Southern Railway* opens up and departs Southampton Docks on the Cunarder Boat Train. The Cunarder in the background is the *Queen Mary*. The final steam-hauled boat train would be hauled by rebuilt Pacific No. 34021, formerly *Dartmoor*, on the final day, 9th July. *Sir Eustace* was built at Brighton in February 1949 and rebuilt at Eastleigh in August 1960. It was allocated to Ramsgate when new. Withdrawn in July 1967, after running 743,948 miles, and broken up at Cashmores Newport in March 1968. Photo taken on 21st June 1967 by Barry J. Eagles.

Standard Class '4' 2-6-0 No. 76061 waits to depart Southampton Terminus with the last steam-hauled train from there; the 16.02 'stopper' to Bournemouth. A small plaque can be seen on the front running plate commemorating this significant event. Although the station was closed that night, the running lines from Northam Jct to the Eastern Docks were retained for Docks traffic. No. 76061 was built at Doncaster in July 1955 and allocated to the Southern Region. Withdrawn in January 1967 from Eastleigh shed, and broken up at Cashmores, Newport in June 1967. Photo taken on 3rd September 1966 by Barry J Eagles.

'West Country' Pacific No. 34093 *Saunton* passes Ashurst Crossing with the 'up' Channel Island boat train. *Saunton* was built at Brighton in October 1949, and rebuilt at Eastleigh in May 1960. She was allocated to Bournemouth Shed when new. *Saunton* worked until the end of steam, and on the evening of 7th July 1967 was in charge of the last 5.23pm weekdays Waterloo to Bournemouth train. Withdrawn in July 1967, after running 888,004 miles and broken up at Cashmores Newport in March 1968. Photo taken on 5th June 1967 by Barry J. Eagles.

Standard Class '4' 2-6-0 No. 76007 passes under Battledown flyover with a train for Salisbury. No. 76007 was built at Horwich in January 1953, one of the ten Standard Class '4' 2-6-0s that worked until the end of Southern steam. Withdrawn in July 1967 and broken up at Birds Risca in November 1967. Nos. 76017, 76077, 76079 and 76084 are preserved. Photo taken on 9th June 1967 by Barry J. Eagles.

Above: Standard Class '4' 4-6-0 No. 75074 flashes past Ashurst Crossing with an 'up' stopping train. No. 75074 was built at Swindon in November 1955, and fitted with a double chimney in July 1961. Built new for the Southern Region, 75074 was withdrawn in July 1967 from Eastleigh shed. She was broken up at Kings Norwich.
Photo taken on 5th June 1967 by Barry J. Eagles.

Right: Standard Class '4' 4-6-0 No. 75075 is neatly framed by trees and giant mole hills as she heads a stopping train near Ashurst Crossing. No. 75075 was built at Swindon in November 1955. Built new for the Southern Region, she was fitted with a double chimney in September 1961. Withdrawn in July 1967 and broken up at Kings Norwich.
Photo taken on 21st June 1967 by Barry J. Eagles.

Left: Bulleid 'Battle of Britain' Pacific No. 34087 *145 Squadron* races past Ashurst Crossing with an 'up' express. *145 Squadron*'s details are on page 49. Photo taken on 16th June 1967 by Barry J. Eagles.

Above: Standard Class '4' 2-6-0 No. 76066 passes the site of Nursling Station with a Banana Train from Southampton Docks. Bananas would be bound for a ripening shed at Avonmouth, and had to be carried in special steam heated vans. No. 76066 was built at Doncaster in July 1956 and allocated to the Southern Region. Eastleigh Shed was her home for most of her working life. Withdrawn in July 1967 and broken up at Cohens Morriston in November 1967. Photo taken on 14th June 1967 by Barry J. Eagles.

'West Country' Pacific No. 34018 *Axminster* receives attention at Nine Elms Engine Shed. Nine Elms towards the end of steam was a shadow of its former self, becoming increasingly untidy, indeed it lost its allocation of ten 'Merchant Navy' Pacifics to Weymouth in the January, although seven of them were sent back to Nine Elms for the end in July. *Axminster* was built at Brighton in December 1945 and allocated to Exmouth Junction Shed. She was rebuilt at Eastleigh in October 1958. Withdrawn at the end of Southern Steam in July 1967 after running 974,317 miles and broken up at Cashmores, Newport in April 1968. Photo taken on 16th July 1964 by Barry J. Eagles.

'West Country' Pacific No. 34036 *Westward Ho* proudly sports the Union Castle Line's headboard at Nine Elms Engine Shed. The block of flats bring home the suburban district feel of south London. The area these days is of course the site of Nine Elms Market. *Westward Ho* was built at Brighton in July 1946 and allocated to Stewarts Lane Shed. Rebuilt at Eastleigh in September 1960. Withdrawn at the end of Southern Steam in July 1967 after running 894,546 miles and broken up at Cashmores, Newport in February 1968. *Westward Ho* worked the 'up' 'Bournemouth Belle' on the 5th July 1967, which was the very last steam-hauled Belle. Photo taken on 16th July 1964 by Barry J. Eagles.

'Merchant Navy' Pacific No. 35008 *Orient Line* climbs past Upwey Wishing Well Halt with a parcels train from Weymouth. *Orient Line* was built at Eastleigh in June 1942. Mr I.C. Geddes Chairman of Orient Line named her at Waterloo Station on 2nd November 1942. She was allocated when new to Salisbury Shed, and rebuilt at Eastleigh in May 1957. *Orient Line* had her nameplates restored for working the official Southern Region's Farewell to Steam Tour on the 2nd July 1967. She worked eleven coaches from Waterloo to Weymouth. Withdrawn in July 1967 after running 1,286,448 miles and broken up at Buttigiegs Newport in October 1968. Photo taken on 10th June 1967 by Barry J. Eagles.

Standard Class '5' 4-6-0 No. 73092 brings a Waterloo bound express under the road bridge near Hinton Admiral. The Christchurch road over the line looked busy even thirty-five years ago! With just one month to go for full electrification, the third rails are fully in place. No. 73092 details are on page 6. Photo taken on 10th June 1967 by Barry J. Eagles.

'Merchant Navy' Pacific No. 35030 *Elder Dempster Lines* heads a 'down' express for Bournemouth near Walkford. *Elder Dempster Lines* details are on page 31. Photo taken on 10th June 1967 by Barry J. Eagles

'Merchant Navy' Pacific No. 35028 *Clan Line,* with nameplates restored, heads the second of the two official Southern Region's Farewell Tours up Sway Bank. *Clan Line*'s details are on page 12. Photo taken on 2nd July 1967 by Barry J. Eagles.

Above: 'Merchant Navy' Pacific No. 35011 *General Steam Navigation*, in a filthy condition waits to depart from Waterloo. *General Steam Navigation* was built at Eastleigh in December 1944 and allocated to Nine Elms Shed. Mr R. Kelso, Chairman of *General Steam Navigation* named her at Waterloo Station on the 20th February 1945. *General Steam Navigation* was rebuilt at Eastleigh in July 1959. Withdrawn in February 1966 after running 1,069,128 miles. Bought by Woodham Brothers of Barry and after 22 years of storage bought for preservation. Reputed to be the only steam locomotive, with the word steam in its name. Photo taken on 10th August 1965 by Barry J. Eagles.

Right top: 'Merchant Navy' Pacific No. 35030 *Elder Dempster Lines*, shares the limelight with Standard Class '3' 2-6-2 tank No. 82020 at Waterloo Station. No. 82020 was built at Swindon in August 1954, one of a class of 45 engines built there. Allocated to the London Midland Region when new. Transferred to the Western Region and finally to the Southern at Nine Elms in April 1965. Withdrawn in September 1965 and broken up at Birds Risca in January 1966. For details on No. 35030 see page 31. Photo taken on 6th June 1965 by Barry J. Eagles.

Right bottom: Shortly after the above shot, No. 82020 departs Waterloo with empty coaching stock, bound for Clapham Junction carriage sidings. These engines used a boiler based on the standard Swindon No. 2 boiler. Photo taken on 6th June 1965 by Barry J. Eagles.

Standard Class '3' 2-6-0 No. 77014 heads away from Totton with a stopping train for Bournemouth. No. 77014 was built at Swindon in June 1954, one of a class of 20 engines. Most of her life was spent in the North Eastern Region, but she came south in March 1966 to work a railtour and never went back. Allocated to Guildford shed and withdrawn in July 1967. No. 77014 was broken up at Birds Risca; none of the class is preserved.
Photo taken on 13th March 1967 by D.M. Cox

'The morning after the night before'. Three Bulleid Pacifics share the interior of Nine Elms shed shortly after the end of steam on 9th July 1967. No. 35023, formerly *Holland Afrika Line*, took part in the last few day's events by hauling the 8.30am Waterloo to Weymouth train on the 8th July 1967 which was the last steam-hauled 'up' Channel Islands Boat Train. Ex drivers and firemen would help preserve the Unrebuilt on the far left - No. 34023 *Blackmore Vale*, which was bought in a block purchase from British Railways along with *Clan Line* and Ivatt tank No. 41298. Apart from photographers catching the scene, artists such as David Shepherd were well-known for painting this somewhat depressing view.
Photograph courtesy of Roger Hardingham Collection.